Map Scales

By Mary Dodson Wade

Consultant
Jeanne Clidas, Ph.D.
National Reading Consultant
and
Professor of Reading, SUNY Brockport

SCHOLASTIC INC.

New York Toronto London Auckland Sydney
Mexico City New Delhi Hong Kong Buenos Aires

Designer: Herman Adler Design
Photo Researcher: Caroline Anderson
The artwork on the cover shows a simple map and corresponding scale.

ISBN 0-516-24803-0

12 11 10 9 8 7 6 5 4 3 2   4 5 6 7 8/0

Printed in the U.S.A.   61

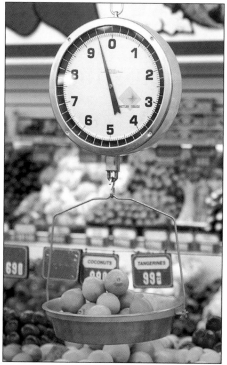

There are scales on fish
and scales for weighing
(WAY-ing) fruit. What kind
of scales do maps have?

3

Maps have scales that help you read the map.

The map scale helps you measure (MEZH-ur) how far away something is.

The scale is a line that stands for a certain distance (DISS-tuhnss).

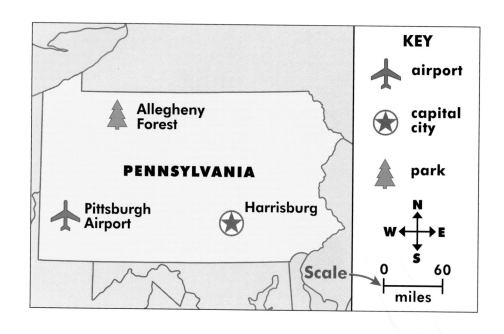

KEY

✈ airport

⊛ capital city

🌲 park

N
W ← → E
S

Scale → 0 ——— 60
miles

Allegheny Forest

PENNSYLVANIA

Pittsburgh Airport

Harrisburg

5

MAP KEY

 airport

 capital city

 park

0   60

miles

Every map has a map scale line. The line is located inside a box called a map key or legend (LEG-uhnd). The legend can be found on the side, top, or bottom of the map.

Also inside the map key box are symbols (SIM-buhlz). These symbols stand for places on the map.

Where is the airport on this map?

Trees show where a park can be found.

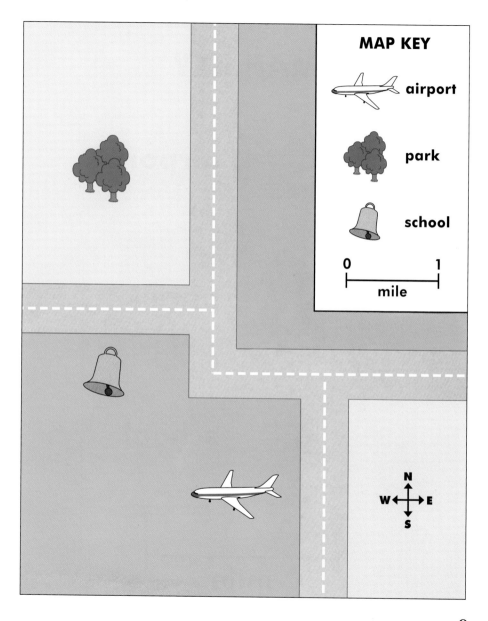

MAP KEY

airport

park

school

0   1
mile

N
W   E
S

9

MAP KEY

airport

park

school

0   1

mile

The distance covered by the map scale line changes with each map. This scale line stands for one mile.

On a map of a country, the line might stand for 200 miles.

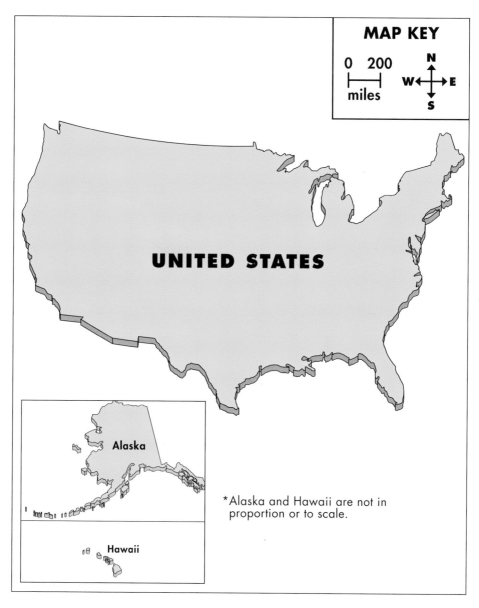

MAP KEY

0　200
⊢————⊣
miles

N
W ←✛→ E
S

UNITED STATES

Alaska

Hawaii

*Alaska and Hawaii are not in proportion or to scale.

13

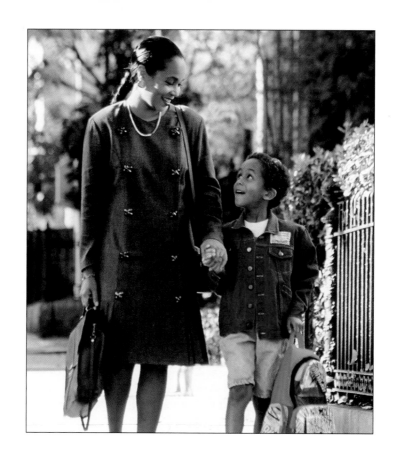

On a map of the block
where you live, the line
might stand for 40 feet.

When you read a map,
look at the map scale line.
Do you see the number at
the end of the line? It
shows how many feet or
miles the line stands for.

0 | **200**

miles

0 | **40**

feet

Little marks divide up the line. These marks show shorter distances.

Here is a map of a zoo.
Find the giraffe's house
and the polar bear's
swimming pool.

Use your ruler to measure
the map scale line. It is
one inch long.

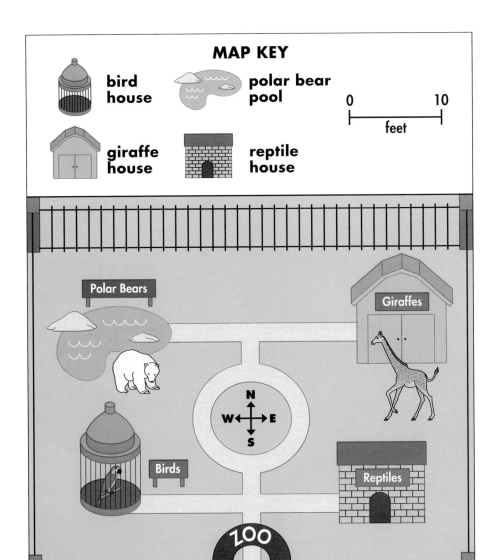

MAP KEY

bird house

polar bear pool

giraffe house

reptile house

0 ━━━━━━━━ 10
feet

Polar Bears

Giraffes

N
W ← → E
S

Birds

Reptiles

ZOO

21

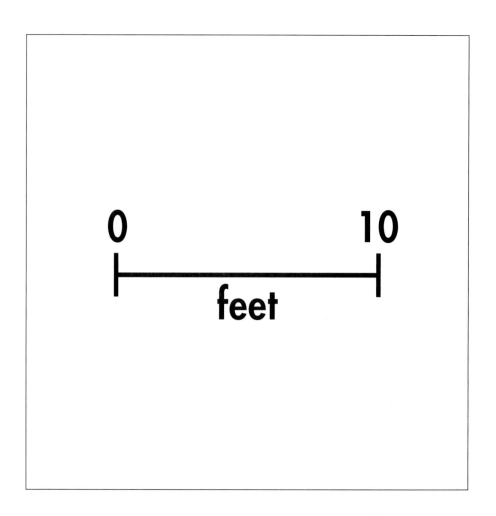

Now look at the number at the end of the map scale line. It shows you that one inch stands for 10 feet.

How far is the giraffe's house from the polar bear's pool?

Use your ruler to measure the distance. Did you measure two inches?

The giraffe's house and the polar bear's pool are two inches apart on the map.

How far apart are they at the zoo?

Add 10 feet plus 10 feet and you will know the distance between the giraffe's house and the polar bear's pool.

Answer: 20 feet

A map scale helps you figure out the distance between places on a map.

How can this help you?

Words You Know

giraffe

map key

map

map scale line

polar bear

ruler

park

school

symbols

Index

About the Author

Mary Dodson Wade spent 25 years as an elementary school teacher, but she has been writing even longer than that, starting with poems as a child. She has had more than 20 books published. Mary and her husband live in Houston, Texas, and love to travel.

Photo Credits